SYSTEMATIC

How to get out of the system mindset.

ANTONIO D. SHERRELL

The contents of this work including, but not limited to, the accuracy of events, people, and places depicted; opinions expressed; permission to use previously published materials included; and any advice given or actions advocated are solely the responsibility of the author, who assumes all liability for said work and indemnifies the publisher against any claims stemming from publication of the work.

All Rights Reserved
Copyright © 2021 by Antonio D. Sherrell

No part of this book may be reproduced or transmitted, downloaded, distributed, reverse engineered, or stored in or introduced into any information storage and retrieval system, in any form or by any means, including photocopying and recording, whether electronic or mechanical, now known or hereinafter invented without permission in writing from the publisher.

RoseDog Books
585 Alpha Drive, Suite 103
Pittsburgh, PA 15238
Visit our website at *www.rosedogbookstore.com*

ISBN: 978-1-4809-8059-4
eISBN: 978-1-4809-8082-2

TABLE OF CONTENTS

DEDICATION

This book is dedicated to my dad, my hero. Your spirit continues to live through me.

ABOUT THE BOOK

This book aims to break the shackles of our overdependence on systems or institutions —like work, religion, school, and criminal justice system, and expose how they confine or limit us from maximizing our God-given potentials. This book also gives direction on how to change that mindset.

The inspiration to write this book was borne out of my personal experiences in life. I categorize the journey of my life into two parts: systemic validation and post-systemic validation. I spent a quantifiable part of my life following conventions and bowing to bandwagonism—systemic validation, until I got to a point when I was determined to break free and chart my course (Post-systemic Validation). They are the many structures that have become burdens to us. We need to identify and let go of them.

Writing this book wasn't a smooth ride. I woke up on a Saturday morning at 5am as if something was pulling at me, telling me to write. I began to write until I wrote almost a whole book. In the process, I started with 'thinking outside the box' to create a more fulfilled life. It was as if I had a direct download from God. Then I hit a block (self-doubt) for a while. I began to think about the acceptability of what I wrote. Questions like "What if people don't like it" or "What if it causes controversy" began to fill my mind until one day, I went into my office and closed the door to pray (my everyday ritual). After I was done, I turned on a YouTube video talking about the very thing I was writing about; not depending on 'The System.' This was the confirmation I needed.

This book encourages people to think outside of the four walls of their office building and schools — and see that there is more to life than punching the clock every day. Life is a lot more fun than investing decades into a company that has not reciprocated the gesture, and will most likely, never do. Success in life for young adults doesn't have to involve piling up thousands of dollars in debt just to go to college. This book gives hope to people who have been exposed to negativity, trauma, and poverty all their lives — hence they have come to believe that it's their only path. I encourage you to look within yourself every day and not in the system, to see that you are a creator, and you can do anything you want. Dream big! Stop settling! Take a chance, and stop taking the safe way out because of the fear of failure. If you decide what you want and devise a lucid plan, life is waiting for you to manifest all your dreams.

ABOUT ME

I grew up in Detroit — a city with an infamous reputation for crime and violence. Even in this, I was fortunate enough to enjoy a good upbringing. This was only possible because of my father's hard work and unwinding vision of ensuring that his family experiences a better life than he did as a youth. Thankfully, his efforts towards us are beginning to yield dividends. Currently, I live in Atlanta with my beautiful wife and son. We are both working toward success in our careers. I work in the social service field as an advocate and she is an attorney. One of my goals is to help youths maximize their potential by reducing the juvenile recidivism rate through education and mentorship. And my other goal is to carry on the Sherrell (my family name) legacy and make my dad proud as he would have wanted. Ultimately, I believe everyone's goal should be related to this, in one way. By this, I mean using your gifts to create wealth while you're on earth and leaving an inheritance for future generations of your family. In the bible, Proverb 13:22 says "*A good man leaves an inheritance for his children's children, but the wealth of the sinner is stored up for the righteous*". Sinning also means not doing everything we can to fulfill our potentials. Also, as Oprah would say, *"be the best version of the greatest vision you've ever had of yourself."*

MY JOURNEY SO FAR

My parents did an awesome job raising me and my siblings, and I will forever adulate them for it. They loved and provided for us, which included putting us in good schools in order to give us a good chance of being successful in life. They also disciplined us when necessary, even though we never liked it. We lived in a good neighborhood but the perception of Detroit was, if you make it out alive, and not in prison, you've done well. And since I was able to go to college on a football scholarship and graduate, I was seen as successful even though I always wanted more.

I was a smart kid but I didn't always maximize my potential. I worked enough in order to achieve and sustain success. My grades were not the best in high school or in college. This is partly because I put more time into sports and leisure than I did my academics. I started off college majoring in electrical engineering but I later switched my major to criminal justice. After failing to make it to the NFL, I quickly realized I had to move on with my life and start providing for myself as a young adult, especially as my parents had already cut me off. My first job was at a group home working with youths in the legal system about 30 minutes from my apartment in Saginaw, MI. At the time, I thought it was just a job but, I soon realized God had something bigger in store in for me. I chose that job because I enjoyed my sociology classes, working at kids camps and reading to the elementary school kids with my football teammates. These were some of Detroit's roughest kids. I learned a lot about kids and myself during this time.

I still felt a void in my life because I hadn't really pursued a career in the NFL. After I moved to Atlanta with my ex-girlfriend, I gave it another shot. I participated in pro-football combine which resulted in me signing with an arena football team. Arena football is an indoor professional football league on a lower level than the NFL. I had a short stint playing arena football in Florida and South Georgia. However, I believed I had scratched my football itch enough to where I was ready to move on with my life. I had overcome my first major systemic confinement: The Need to play in the NFL to be considered successful. For someone who got a football scholarship through college, It was difficult giving up on the sport, but I did what had to be done. I broke the convention. I was ready to start my career and my put my degree to use. I've always been about accomplishing goals and overcoming obstacles, but moving to Atlanta was the first big step for me because I had never lived out of the state before. When I moved, I had little money and no job, so I was really taking a leap of faith. Sometimes you have absolutely no idea where your path is taking you, so all you need to do is just have faith. I had the feeling that my parents were upset with me for moving without a real plan. While I respected their opinions and understood their reticence towards my plan, I felt unperturbed in the pursuit of the course I chose for myself and I was not going to look back.

Another major systemic confinement I overcame was religion. I was raised and baptized in the church as a kid. I also attended a Catholic school from 4th grade to high school. As you can imagine, I had a fair share of participation in church activities, an understanding of religion and a moral foundation to lean on as an adult. However, I always secretly questioned the unconscious ways with which the church limited God to a place. I have always opined that the church, and religion as a whole, should major on teachings that exposes us to the unlimited potentials we possess when we allow God to operate in us. Even the bible, which contains the modus operandi of the church, corroborates my point in 1 John 4:4: *"Greater is he that is in me, than he that is in world".*

I believe in the efficacy of prayers. I strongly attribute many successes and breakthrough enjoyed by my family, especially during difficult periods, to the workability of prayers. But the pattern of going to God when times are hard and paying tithes, or giving offerings to religious leaders, when many people around are struggling financially, was sometimes difficult for me to understand. Call me naïve, but I thought life immediately changes when you followed this script. However, I learned through much trials and errors that there was more to it than just following the script. Instead of just going to the house of God to get an understanding of God from the preacher, I decided to go to God myself. I invested a lot of my time reading the bible more than I ever did. My view of God began to seem different. I viewed God as an unlimited being that didn't focus on petty things such as how often we go to church or how often one pays his tithes or just attend bible study. The God I was exposed to, in my deep perusal of the bible, doesn't have time to focus only on things like that. Personally, I feel God is focused more on helping us discover the power we have to change the world. Just like it was recorded in the bible, Jesus told the disciples: *"whoever believes in me will do the works I have been doing and they will do even greater things than these."* I don't understand this (religion, for example, is a big one). This bible aims to bring people to the realization of the fact that there are no limitations with God. I pointed out for people to understand that religiosity alone cannot take you through life successfully. When church services or any other religious activities are over, you still have to believe in yourself, you still have to work hard, experience life to the fullest and trust the process to make significant progress. There are no shortcuts. I am reminding you to believe in yourself because we often forget that we are and have everything we need to be great because we were created in God's likeness and image.

Limitation was another systemic confinement I got over in my journey in life. I wasn't focused on a vision, goal or purpose for my life— which resulted in me participating in unfulfilled relationships. I wasn't strategic enough. When I worked at a Group Home in LaGrange, GA., I worked several hours a week to make ends meet and party— my mind and thinking was limited to merely the basics that I didn't have time for what was important. I hadn't yet understood the importance of finding a purpose and setting goals that align with it. My parents instilled hard work within us at an early age by giving us chores like cutting the grass, cleaning the house and doing the dishes. My brother and I also helped my dad renovate properties. The time came when I wanted to settle down. I wanted a house, a family and children, but I didn't think I made enough money to achieve my goal. I decided to take another leap of faith and purchased a house. I was stepping out on faith because I believed that I would have a home and soon after start a family. Since faith without works is dead I added hard work to my vision until it became a reality. Shortly after, my dream of owning a home came true and soon after that, I was getting married and starting a family. When it was time to pay the closing cost, I had no idea where I was going to get the money but, out of nowhere, my friend said *"I will help you out with the money you need for the down payment on your house."* That friend would later become my wife. While this might be rightly categorized as a sort of miracle, I had to take a step to defeat the structural confinement of limitation that held me bound for years by preventing me from thinking I could even own a house.

THE IDEA OF THE SYSTEM

Sometime ago, I found myself seated in my study, in absolute decorum, thinking about my life and that of my friends and loved ones. It resulted in a mirage of mixed feelings. I thought of how many of my friends were grateful for their families, homes, and jobs but still wanted more out of life. Some of them were cautious of their ambitions, as they didn't want to be seen as unappreciative of what they already have, just like many people around today. It seemed rather funny to me. It felt like we are being guilt-tripped into bending to the convention of a system —that which demonizes one for being ambitious and competitive. According to renowned author, Alan Watts, "Society does not need more religion. We need to experience life to the fullest." Religion here doesn't have to be Christianity or Islam — it is any system that is very intolerant of fluidity. Don't get me wrong, this is not to undervalue the importance of processes in our lives. These systems only become one because they have been seen, more often than not, to be a suitable approach or style by a preponderance of people. I am not, in any way, advocating for religion or any systemized process to be discountenanced. In fact, I believe that in life, you can never find your proper direction without going through the process — but some never wake up and find the right direction. Many operate under the same traditional mindset, afraid to think outside the normal spectrum of school, work and religion.

Some religious folks have created a false image of God in their subconscious. They now propagate him as an unforgiving and ego-driven ruler. They see him as someone who watches our every move and is going to brutally punish anyone who doesn't meet his standards or questions him for wanting more than the basics. Even when the bible says “my God shall supply all my needs according to his riches in glory” —some people are still afraid that God would disapprove them for wanting better or more out of life.

I believe that this point of view is more of a figment of the limited imagination of man than the true desire of an all-powerful God. However, throughout history, religion has played a major role in making us feel guilty for thinking for ourselves and believing that we are worthy and capable of greatness. Also, there is a huge dichotomy with many in regards to religion because religion was the powerful tool used to keep many in bondage, yet many people continue to stay confined by the traditional ideologies of religion. I believe the true God wants us to embody his power and act as such because scripture says we were made in his likeness and image. What I take from that scripture, is not that we can judge or strike down those who do us wrong, but that we are creators like God who created us. We can think, believe, speak and create the lives we want just like he did when he created us — his most powerful creation— and the magnificent vast universe. Christ also operated in his highest purpose — his maximum potential — according to the records in the bible. He believed in this purpose so much that he was willing to die for it. Furthermore, I want you to understand that if your purpose is aligned with God, it will not come from a selfish perspective — it will serve as a blessing to others. Therefore it is almost guaranteed to come to fruition.

God is not a fan of limitation. I'm not sure about you, but for me success means enjoying life to the fullest. These include financial freedom, success, wealth, philanthropy and leaving a great legacy for my family

I call these institutions created by society '*The System*'. Some of us place our full trust, and search for fulfillment, in them. Why not trust the powerful being inside us? *Systems* were created by man, and they are subject to failure and corruptness. Why then do we still continue to solely rely on them? Why not take a chance on yourself. Believe in yourself!

First, you have to think different than you were taught. There is more to life. Then you have to dare to dream. Once you begin to dream, you realize this is your reality that has not been manifested yet. When we don't change, eventually we lie dormant— inactive, stagnant, shiftlessness—culminating to our expiration. Mr. Watts states, "Since life has no meaning and he sees no future life, he is no longer a person but a victim of self-extinction" (*On the Taboo of Knowing Who You Are, pg.17*). Before you can go to another level, you must have a shift in thinking.

THE CRIMINAL JUSTICE SYSTEM

The criminal justice system is an unending cycle of problems. It seems like once a person is involved with the system— there is no way out. Prisoners, who might be guilty of committing a specific crime, have their life almost ruined because they become directionless when they get out. Nobody wants to hire a convicted felon who has no education or skill. This is why they usually go back to what they seemingly know best — committing crimes— which will inadvertently send them back to jail or prison. If the felon finally does get their life on track, the negative environment, which is not conducive for growth, usually pulls them back to a life of crime. It's like planting an apple tree in a field full of weeds. You can give it plenty of sunshine and water, but ultimately it will not grow to its full potential because of its environment. More importantly, the person needs to be nurtured from the inside out. Through self-belief and believing in a higher power, they can achieve absolutely anything they set their minds on. You can always rewrite your story if you want to change it and make a difference.

Children are starting off in this system at a very early age, they are charged with minor offenses that places a negative stigma on them. Prison is a billion dollar business. It is also a lot similar to slavery where many of the prisoners provide cheap labor for private industries. More prisons are being built than schools, therefore if it does not make dollars, it doesn't make sense. Societies believe that if some persons do not have any value in the community, then we can get cheap labor from them behind bars where they are also being punished.

I also observed in my experience that some parents seem more relieved when their children are locked up. It's sad that some parents believe their children are better off in jail than they are on the streets. They think like this because they feel they are no longer responsible for what happens to them. Also, the crazy thing is that some people in the criminal justice system receive better shelter, food and medical attention than they would in the community —the system will make you believe that you are being taken care of. Also, it will make you believe that being in bondage, slavery, and confinement is somehow better than being free to create the life you want. People need to understand that freedom also entails freedom within their minds. This means that to be truly free, you have to be able to believe and create whatever you want in life.

Another problem with the criminal justice system is that the streets are raising children while parents are trying to make ends meet. This leaves our children and teenagers vulnerable to become products of the system. Since the incorporation of the criminal Justice system, laws were created to keep the upper class safe from the lower class—specifically minorities or African-Americans and Hispanic people. In the era of slave trade, African-Americans were viewed as second class citizens, initially considered 3/5 of a person. The minority population in America is populated by the African-American and Hispanic race. This demographic is presumed guilty before actually committing a crime— because they were never considered equal to the majority in the first place. Instead of allowing African-Americans to live their lives like normal citizens, who work hard towards thriving in society, the system prefer to have them placed behind bars— where they can get free labor which is a form of slavery. I'm sure you've heard the term, 'crime pays' — well, it sure does for the wealthy.

History is clear as to how white supremacy, over the years, has culminated to violence and maltreatment of the minority. Since Prisons are funded by many wealthy corporations such as banks. Lobbyists, in turn, vote for certain laws and policies that maximize the profitability of prisons for the owners. This means that they support laws that increase the chances of more people getting jailed. The more the prisoners, the more free labor and the more the rich get richer. In order to keep the prisons filled with minorities, the lobbyist will continue pushing for new laws that catalyzes it. As with slavery, many businesses and investors are profiting from the prison industry because it's a sure return on their investment. Lastly, studies show the recidivism rate (the rate at which convicted criminals reoffend) is reduced by 70% when one is educated with at least a high school education. Now, the question I ask is, why is the government not pushing for more education rather than stricter laws and harsher prison sentences? Why is there no push to shift from the conventional practice?

Poverty is another important part of being trapped in the criminal justice system. Two-parent homes are important as well— as one strong parent can pick up the other with hard work. Poverty inhibits the success of children. This is because these kids don't have the strong family support system. And as such, they are susceptible to negative environmental factors that impact their growth such as poor education, poor feeding and healthcare, hooliganism and crime, drug abuse, etc. All of these negative factors, which are mostly not faults of theirs, almost surely lead these kids to jail. I was at risk of falling into the system. However, I was blessed to have strong parental figures —other important figures such as grandparents, aunts, uncles, coaches and mentors as well— to caution me. What I have for you is that your circumstances do not determine your outcome. Do not believe the statistics that almost condemns you because of your neighborhood or because of how you grew up. Statistics are just mere postulations from previous occurrences. They do not have to be right. You can completely break free from the negative statistics propounded against you and your kind if you decide to deviate from the system that has been holding you down. The god within you has the final determination as to what you will become in life. So, stop following the bandwagon, and stop listening to the naysayers because you are more powerful than you think. It will take one determined person who is unabated in his convictions to fuel the need for a holistic criminal justice reform.

In 2012, 16 year old unarmed African-American male Trayvon Martin was murdered by George Zimmerman while walking in a suburb with a hoody on and skittles in his possession. Zimmerman was not a law enforcement officer, he was a citizen patrolling the neighborhood and thought a young black male with a hoody on was up to no good. A scuffle ensued after Zimmerman approached Martin with no merit, resulting in Zimmerman shooting Martin once Martin got the best of him. More importantly, Zimmerman was not convicted. Trayvon's murder sparked the Black Lives Matter movement. Long before Trayvon's murder and thereafter have been many other unarmed African-Americans who were murdered by law enforcement officers, lynched and shot with little to no explanation or conviction. This goes back to the point that we cannot depend on a flawed, outdated, biased and unjust criminal justice system. There needs to be reformation to include fairness and justice for all. There is a popular African adage that says: *'You cannot do the same thing repeatedly and expect a different result'.*

THE SAFE WAY OUT (9-5)

Working a 9-5, at most jobs, usually come with some enticing packages. They include health benefits, 401k, vacations, sick leave and many more depending on the affluence of your organization. However, you can enjoy all these and many more, without depending solely on a job, if you allow your money to work for you. Allowing your money work for you, in this sense, is not limited to investments. It cuts across everything that involves making money on your own without depending on salaries from jobs. What skills do you have? What can you learn at your job that can be of advantage to you? Every employee should have these questions at the back of their minds while they do their 9-5. Time is money, so making your money work for you also includes gaining valuable experience from your jobs even as you get paid. A 9-5 becomes a training ground for you as you plan to become your own boss.

In many societies, people work from hands to mouth and, strangely, have become comfortable with it. It seems extremely difficult for many people to go outside of their comfort zone and put in the extra time to accomplish their dreams. Similar to the criminal justice system and college, people are now conformed to having someone tell them what to do all through their lives. These are the same people complaining, yet they refuse to do anything about it. Perhaps, it's the other way around. Not pursuing what fulfills you, not doing what you're passionate about or what makes you happy is the root of unhappiness. Working at a job only because it pays the bills doesn't sound rewarding. The goal of any company is to maximize profit. This will mean that they pay you the minimum amount of money for your services and the get maximum production out of you. You become dependent to where you feel like that's the only work you're capable of performing. Then you feel like it's too late because it's too close to retirement. You've already invested

10+ years to this company, so you feel like you may as well stay the next 20 years.

The company views you as being expendable; they will find another worker just like you. Don't place too much extra time and energy into the job because it is just a job. Even though different studies have shown that employees do not give their best in a 9-5 system, nothing has changed. Why? Your guess is as good as mine. The system is designed to discourage employees from focusing on their passion. The 9-5 ecosystem also consists of part-time workers who shuffle two to three jobs daily to meet ends meet. This is even worse than conventional jobs because it comes with almost no valuable experience and very little remuneration. These set of people work almost all day through their active years and retire with almost nothing to fall back on when you factor in the cost of inflation with only a percentage of the income you once earned.

There is no doubt that there are a plethora of genuine excuses as to why it's impossible to focus on your passion in the system we operate. But the truth is that we will always find time for things that we feel are important. I suggest you put that extra time into figuring out your passion. People are also afraid of change. It's easier to stay comfortable as opposed to trying something new and interesting— that could possibly compensate you better and is more fulfilling. People who are striving for success understand that things are going to get difficult before they get better. Successful people are willing to go through uncomfortable times before reaching success. Don't ever believe that your life is over because you're at a dead end job. Never count yourself out, always believe in yourself and most importantly believe in God.

Always remember that you are the vessel that God chose for a greater purpose. We have to understand that the kingdom of God is within all of us. We choose to continue to play small, not knowing that God is waiting for us to do something big— so he can intervene and show you why he is the all-powerful supreme God. Of course, we can accomplish things on our own, but when God is involved, it becomes a big deal. We are not taking advantage of the gifts and opportunities we have been given. Therefore, we die a less meaningful death without fulfilling our purpose on earth. Less brown said the richest place on Earth is the cemetery. His rationale was based on the view that most people die without pursuing their true passion or purpose in life. This is the only life you have, so take advantage of it. Make time after work or in your spare time to tap into your gifts.

All successful people use their gifts and talents to bring them happiness, fulfillment, riches, wealth and success, i.e. Oprah Winfrey's gift of speaking, Bill Gates' knowledge of computer software, Warren Buffet's knowledge of business, and Mark Zuckerberg,s knowledge of people. We all have gifts, things that come natural to us—things that we're passionate about and would do for free. However, some of us are not aware of the presence of these gifts. Your job is important to you temporarily, but what is your plan for the long term? How are you putting your gifts to use? Lastly, everyone is not meant to be entrepreneurs, business owners, entertainers, athletes, millionaires or billionaires. You can be blessed and fulfilled working a 9-5 too. The same goes for the statement everyone is not meant to work a 9-5.

Honestly, it takes a disciplined, strong, committed and dedicated person to work at one job for 30 plus years. In spite of that, you should not limit yourself to a 9-5, if you believe your gifts can be put to greater use. Many entrepreneurs and business owners continue working their 9-5 until their business or businesses begin to thrive. You can also stay at yours and generate passive residual income doing something you're passionate about as well. Everyone is capable of greatness. God did not assign it to a few people. Take out time today from your multitude of jobs to breathe. Ruminate on your passion and drive. Concretize a plan. Dedicate some hours of your time to nurture this vision and watch it grow on the sideline. The 10 dollars forgone won't make or mar you. Look at the bigger picture. Will Smith said, *"You too are capable of greatness now go find your purpose"*. *N*ow go and find your purpose.

RELIGION

Religion is a major part of the system. Like I briefly stated in the About the Book section, I had to fight to break through the system. It wasn't an easy fight, I must say, especially as someone who was brought up in a Christian home. Instead of people thinking for themselves, they have become heavily dependent on religious structures to think for them. For example, when you attend classes in school or college, you listen to the instructor to obtain the lesson which is good. However, reading the book yourself helps to internalize the information better. This is because you're getting the information from the source. Reading religious books and obtaining the information yourself strengthens your faith, knowledge and understanding of the religion. Listening to religious leaders is also very useful, they are knowledgeable instructors teaching the word, but we should always remember that they are not the source. Often times, what happens with most people is that they get the teacher confused with the source. You are able to educate yourself with the same information as the teacher because you have direct access to the source. When it's time to spread our wings, we should let go and fly without fear. Fear is always going to be there, but we should still continue to progress. The acronym for fear could mean two things; 'Forget everything and run' or 'Face everything and rise'. Your own interpretation depends on the actions you take. For most people, their spiritual and moral foundations are hinged on religion. Nevertheless, spirituality is not based on religion — it is based on the connection with your inner being. Religion is also spiritual, but it is limited to the laws in the religious books. With laws and religion, there's a sense of accountability and also damnation. With spiritually, there is an aligned connection or deeper understanding that keeps us on track always. Galatians 3:5 says, "*So again I ask, does God give you his spirit and work miracles among you by works of the law or by your believing what you heard?*" If we depend on law or religion for our moral guide, then we are not trusting the spirit.

Allowing religion to be your only source of moral guidance is hinging your chemistry with God on religious gatherings and offerings. Anyway, I believe that we are connected to God in all things. Even the bible which Christians follow says that *"All things work for the good of those that love God, they too are called according to his purpose."* This doesn't, in any way, invalidate the place of sin and its consequences. The point is that the spirit in man will guide and protect him from sin — which usually culminates into self-condemnation. You should also understand that the kingdom of God is within us and there is no condemnation. Thinking outside of the religious laws teaches people to believe in the God within themselves — rather than the God inside a building. We were made in the likeness and image of God, therefore, we should operate as gods by creating a loving magnificent world. Understanding that God dwells in us is the key, but we have to activate that higher power through prayer, meditation, faith and actions. Once we realize the power we have, the next step would be to act on the visions God placed in us. I know that he was within me when I struggled in high school but still graduated and received a scholarship. He was there when I struggled in college but, ultimately graduated. He was with me during the tough relationships, financial struggles, career struggles and near death accidents, but still made sure I came out of those situations alive. During those times, I had a relationship with God, even though it was not strong. My conscious effort into personal research and internalization concretized my beliefs and strengthened my faith. Now, my faith is stronger than ever. I believe without a shadow of a doubt that if he brought me through those times then he will definitely bring me through tough times into magnificent times. And if he did it for me, he will definitely do it for you — we're all his children.

Sartre states, "That being a moral or religious person requires one to deny authentic impulses (everything that makes us human) and allow the will of another person to change one's actions." This is not entirely true, but its validity can be argued. Many people fall for the fear and guilt tactics. It is another way to keep your mind confined and keep you from self-introspection.

Again, people see religion as something to fall back on when all hopes are lost. They are told if they come to gatherings and pay offerings, they would be blessed. If they do otherwise, they are told that they risk the vengeance of God. Some religious leaders are master manipulators and shady businessmen. Sadly, it's the truth we have to admit. In some part of the world, religion has completely turned into business and religious buildings are rather used for business purposes than for spiritual purposes. The level at which the members get exploit with offerings is alarming, all in the name of *"do it for God".* This has led to different meme pictures circulating on the internet. We scroll through these pictures and laugh, but it's the truth. We need to understand that God has purpose for all of us and he will not create inconveniencies for us. In the bible, Matthew 7:7&8 says *"Ask and it shall be given unto you, seek and ye shall find, knock and it shall be opened unto you. For everyone who asks receives; the one who seeks finds; and to the one who knocks, the door will be opened"*. These are the words of God instructing us to come directly to him with our problems. Unfortunately, people sees religious leaders as their only true connection to God. This way, they lose the little fortunes they've gathered while they get exploited and also lose their spiritual connection with God. Don't get me wrong, I didn't say you shouldn't give back to God when you're blessed. You should give back to God but not through exploitations and imposed fees. In fact, I think the best way to give back to God is through charity. Help the poor, give to the needy, provide support to those who needs it, be generous and show kindness to others. This way, you're helping God's projects and he will bless you even more.

Watts goes on to say, "We don't need more religion or a new bible. We need a new experience, a new feeling of what it means to be 'I'. We were made in the image of God, yet we are content to limit God and say thank you for the basic necessities of life; food, clothes and shelter. I am also grateful for those things, but I believe I can do much greater. If we continue to confine and limit God, we will continue to limit ourselves. These basic necessities can be gotten on our own. Enlarge your dreams, think big, and that is when God will step in.

In 2008, while I working as a Juvenile Probation Officer, I met a good friend. Alice was super cool. She was very spiritual and encouraging during the time when I started to lose hope again. I got back into church mode and she was my partner in crime. We were attending different churches.

It was funny because we called it "searching for God and our blessings". We even tried to start our own Bible study group which did not last very long. We were constantly chasing God, but nothing was changing. To be fair on us though, it was the system, that society told us to follow, that set these principles. Don't get in trouble, go to church, go to mosque, go to school, graduate from college, find a job, work your way up the corporate ladder, and everything will work out great. That's the American dream. They didn't tell us that we would have to work to pay back student loans and credit card bills for most of your life. Or the only time we would be able to take a real vacation is when tax time comes around. Or that the only other time we could earn some money is when we get a second job or go back to school to further your education only to create more bills. Or that when we go to religious gatherings, we feel good for those two hours only to leave feeling the same as before but with a lighter pocket. I just feel that most fervent believers of religion do so to improve their financial situation amongst other reasons. So, why would you obligate someone who is already enduring financial hardships to pay a fee to God, so to speak? The God I know does not need anything.

Something clicked years ago when I was talking to my friend Rodney in Miami, FL. He said, "Man, we did everything we were supposed to do. We went to school and didn't get into any trouble. We graduated from college. Why are we still struggling?" I was going to church and reading the bible which made me somehow think I was a little better. Then I realized that the problem was not us or God.

God is not a businessman like many preachers make us feel. He doesn't necessarily require our service to religion to shower us with his blessings. He is an all-loving and infinitely merciful God whose desire is to see his children flourish and remain in the path of righteousness. Society will victimize anyone who decides not to follow the bandwagon of bending to the religious system. It can be very hard, but a deep understanding of God and his promises towards your life will catalyze it. Break yourself from the shackles of religion and transcend into the realm of the zero limitation of God. God is not man, hence it is condescending to try to appease him with a set of mundane laws. When we fully come to terms with the gargantuan nature of God and his wishes towards us, we would inadvertently get the required inspiration to begin to think big and plan towards fulfillment in life. The only way to understand this nature of God is by investing your time into creating a personal relationship with him. Take that religious book and read it. Let God speak to you directly. Spend time praying to him. God speaks to his children and he will speak to you.

COLLEGE

Schools encourage their students to further their education to increase their chances of getting better paid jobs. Reality has shown that it is not usually the case. Instead, what is guaranteed is the big burden of paying back student loans for most of your life. Operate from where you are now and figure out your real purpose or passion. Your passion doesn't always have to be attached to a degree, even though attaining a degree is a great accomplishment we should be proud of. School gives you the discipline and basic skills necessary to be successful. Statistics have reported that a college degree increases one's salary by 30,000. This is remarkable. But, this is not enough reason to be limited to a degree.

Great accomplishments, such as a high school and college education, are instrumental in success and increases career options and earning potential. College is a great place to figure out your career path, but you surely don't have to go into debt of thousands of dollars in order to discover your future. There are many successful people such as mark Zuckerberg, the Founder of Facebook, who decided not to complete his college education in order to have enough time to pursue his dreams. Now, he is one of the wealthiest most successful creators of all time. That is because he already had a skill set and plan. Dr. Dre and Jay Z are also typical examples as they are successful multimillionaires in the music industry. You don't need to be attached to a college in order to be educated or create your vision. There is plenty of education in books and this will point you in the right direction once you decide your purpose. The government will have you believe college is the best and only way to figure out your future because it is also one of the most profitable systems in America. It will leave you in a position where you're indebted to the government and the only way out is to work very hard for a long period of time after to pay back the debt. Having a high school diploma or trade can be as important as a college education as long as you know your purpose and have an actionable plan. There are many welders, mechanics and skilled professionals who don't have a college education — but their skill set makes them very valuable to the world. The sooner you know your purpose, the more strategic you become in your actions. Then there wouldn't be the need to spend thousands of dollars on continued college education as a means of reaching your goals. Just like religion, we over rely on this institution, forgetting that we have the power to create our own lives if we discipline ourselves to do the necessary self-development and self-education to find our purpose. Instead, we wait for someone to tell us what to do like programmed robots.

School teaches you more of how to follow orders and be a better employee rather than how to think for yourself and be creators. Constantly, we're rather compelled to make decisions, not for ourselves, but for the pleasure of a higher authority that drives us. This is commonly associated with school and students. School is one of the authorities that forces you make decisions while in the process of modeling you into something. As such, you may experience hardship, stress and a lot of rigorous thinking trying to go through the path that has already been created — instead of being guided to create your own path.

Most students in schools really just want to graduate instead of taking time to go through the learning process. They hardly make use of their imagination, and think independently to achieve the desire results needed to create a path for their respective futures. This is as a result of pressure they have been subjected to by school, forcing them into memorizing and just giving it back in tests or during examination periods. This has been termed *'La cram, La pour'* in some part of the world, which simply means *'Memorize and give it back when asked'*.

As a result of this, quite a huge percentage of school graduates are partially experienced in their field of study, while only a handful are well-experienced or experts. The school should play a vital role in training and guiding students into becoming team players as well as independent thinkers. The level of students' exposure to new innovations has reduced over time because the learning process has completely been modified over the years. The effect of this has commonly resulted into just one answer, *"I really just want to graduate"*, a phrase often used by students.

Discipline and time management are the most important skills — however, we don't have patience to indoctrinate it into ourselves. We'd rather pay to have someone tell us what to do. Four years in college costs an average of $30,000 and this could have been used in investing in self-development and business creation. I would not say it's a total waste because there are great people in positions of leadership— such as doctors, lawyers, judges, businessman— who obtained their education in colleges. Formal education is necessary, but you must never jettison the need to pursue your dream. At the very least, make sure you have your basic education. With that, you will be able to do some number work, hold conversations and think properly and wisely. The objective is to keep you depending on the system and thinking you are getting ahead when you get a degree, when the truth is that you are not. You are still in debt. There are a lot of people I know who have several degrees but are still working to pay student loans. It can be a miserable journey. I also know many people who are book smart but lack common-sense knowledge. Their minds are limited to the classroom and can't function outside of that confinement. They always rush back to school at the slightest opportunity. They feel comfortable there and usually end up becoming professors.

It is a constant cycle of working to pay bills and never getting a chance to enjoy the fruits of your labor. The system wants you to be constantly dependent on them. School is also looked at as something to fall back on. When we don't have anything to fall back on, we have a tendency to push forward. The Black Enterprise magazine posted an article dated June 4th, 2011 where famed actor Denzel Washington gave a commencement speech for his son's alma mater, University of Pennsylvania, in 2011. During his speech, he reflected on how he had started out as a pre-med student at Fordham University and then switched to pre-law, then journalism. Before barely passing, he was asked to take some time off to consider his future due to his 1.8 GPA during the semester. He admitted to the class of 2011 that he had been at his lowest point.

Washington also recalled working in his mother's Mt. Vernon beauty shop for a few months before returning to Fordham, where he finally claimed his calling to the theater and changed his major for the last time. He insisted that the great lessons of his winding academic road—to identify your particular gifts and to persevere in honing them no matter what —were never lost on him.

"I'm sure people have told you to make sure you have something to fall back on," Washington told the graduates. *"I never understood that concept. I don't want to fall back on anything except my faith. If I'm going to fall, I want to fall forward."*

Sharing a story about how Thomas Edison persevered through 1,000 failed inventions before nailing the light bulb, the Oscar and Tony award winner implored students to take risks and embrace failure, continually and without shame.

"You will fail," he said. "Accept it. You will lose. You will embarrass yourself. You will suck at something. I should know. In the acting business, you fail all the time. If you don't fail, you're not even trying. So, you got to get out there and give it your all."

Taking risks, he said, is about being open to life, people, foreign ideas, and new frontiers. He insisted that while this might be frightening at first, it will eventually be rewarding. This is because the chances you take, the people you meet, the people you love, and the faith that you have are what will define you."

In the end, he charged the Class of 2011 with a universally inspiring mission: "Never be discouraged. Never hold back. Give it everything you've got. And when you fall, fall forward." The crowd was on its feet before his final words were out of his mouth. A decade earlier, Washington received a standing ovation when he became the second black male to win an Academy Award in the Best Actor category. I'm guessing this moment was just as meaningful.

What if we are able to change our cultural belief from "people can't be trusted" to "people can be trusted to make decisions that are for the highest good of everyone" This is because they care for, and want to contribute to others and themselves. Where would this new belief take us? How differently would we teach our children? If our foundational cultural belief was that "people can be trusted to make their own decisions," then we would most likely want to support them in being aware of what's most important to them and what they personally value.

To be able to trust people with the choice of making the right decision for themselves and people connected to them, there has to be high measure of Emotional Intelligence enshrined in us. Emotional intelligence ensures that we do the right thing without hurting others. This aspect of our lives is usually completely discountenanced in schools as they major in improving our Intelligence Quotient. While EQ helps us survive in a shapeless world like we have today, IQ only helps us function well in systems. And we all know that a perfect system exists only in utopia. Our children's education should probably include developing their emotional intelligence. This would sustain their ability to make decisions based on how their actions might benefit or impact them and those around them. Sadly, we're not raised to clue into our internal values, or notice whether the consequences of our actions are in harmony with our values. Instead, we are constantly being distracted by external authority telling us what to do. Or we are moved to action by the extrinsic motivation of being threatened by the consequences of disobedience. Imagine being raised in a culture where the kind, caring and competent nature is valued and nurtured and the ability to reason and come up with successful, satisfying choices for EVERYONE concerned is respected.

Take a moment and dream about how different you and society would be if your education, both at home and in school, had focused heavily on supporting you in making decisions in line with your internal guidance. What would it have been like if, through teaching and conversations, you had experiences designed to help nurture these abilities?

So, I advise parents to effect the needed change from their homes. Study your kids and create a habitat, in your home, that allows them express their potentials. It might take a long time before the school system adjusts, but you don't have to wait. Educate your kids to know that formal education is only a process of helping them get a clearer picture of their future and not their future itself. Break the shackle of the school system now. Don't spend all your time focusing on getting good grades while your passion and skills deteriorate.

REPROGRAM YOUR MIND

Be not conformed to this world, but be transformed by the renewing of our minds. Once we understand that we are capable of extraordinary and amazing things, the next step will be to stay focused, formulate a plan, work and stay consistent. We do this by listening to the right things, reading the right books, praying, meditating, affirming and spending time with positive people who encourage us to do better. The right things and books, in this sense, are materials that focus on improving our capacity to produce or innovate. There are many books around written to reduce us to nothing and completely condemn us —this is the time to do away with them. There is no perfect person— what we should focus on is the amplification of our talents and skills instead of wallowing in victimization.

We have been made to believe that being unnecessarily pessimistic about people and their chances is tough love. Many of us have close family and friends who always discourage us — directly or indirectly. We have gotten so accustomed to this that we now feel they are good for us. This is a sad reality amongst a lot of people in today's world. It is true that criticisms are as important as adulations in the journey to attaining high level success, but the unnecessary glorification should not be encouraged. It has eaten deep into our subconscious so much that people now gravitate towards pessimists. You, together with your relationship with God, are the determining factor of your success. Your environment means something, but you are ultimately responsible for your own success. By reprogramming our minds to thinking and believing that we are deserving and worthy of greatness, we send a strong signal to the God and our inner man on our readiness to take up a new challenge. God already knows who you are and what you're capable of, because he created you.

Since we were children at school, at work and church, we were reminded of our shortcomings, faults, inadequacies and sins. At school, after we work hard in the classroom all year, a single test determined whether we were successful or not. In religion, if we do something considered bad or not aligned with the prescribed teachings, we are labeled sinners. And at work, you are also considered unsuccessful when you don't meet certain policy requirements. In the criminal justice system, we are labeled as criminals when we commit an offense. The point is that we are constantly reminded of our failures much more than we are of our successes.

Other important factors in reprogramming our mind are self-development, self-actualization and self-mastery. This requires us putting inspiring and encouraging information into our subconscious. There were points in my life when I was operating at my highest level; I was developing myself spiritually, mentally and physically. I call it the trifecta because there is usually an alignment with your mind, body and soul. When God was communicating with his prophets or people, as recorded in religious and historical accounts, there is no hesitation or doubt in purpose. In most cases, there was strict adherence and obedience to whatever instruction doled out. This is because of the unwavering trust the people had in God. It's when we start doubting God's will for our lives that we fall out of alignment with our purpose. Being in alignment on these three important levels almost guarantees success. Improved spiritually makes one more in tuned with the everyday happenings around you — it's like having receptors or neurotransmitters that make you super sensitive.

God made everyone specially. However, there is a job to be done to do activate this spectrum. For mental growth, there is need for constant reading, enlightenment, education and intellectual conversations. There is also a need to take care of the physically body —it is the vessel that harbors the spirit and mind. Proper diets and regular exercises keep the physical body in shape and provide a conducive environment for the spirit and mind to function appropriately. They are all intertwined, so there is a need to have all of them working optimally in alignment with your purpose. Self-actualization means the realization of one's talent, abilities and potential and self-development is the process by which a person's characters or abilities are gradually developed. You start taking your time more seriously —understanding that you're here on Earth to accomplish a mission. You begin to understand that God has entrusted you with a vision and you have an obligation and duty to see it through.

Self-mastery is self-discipline, focus and consistency in working toward attaining these goals. No one ever said it was going to be easy. If God entrusted you with a purpose, you better believe he has given you the necessary skills and placed the right people in your life to accomplish the mission. Remember, your purpose is everything, so reprogram your mind to get in alignment with it for your life to kick off. In the famous movie, 'The Matrix', Neo had different programs downloaded into him, which caused him to be an expert martial artist. But even at that, he was not unstoppable until he believed so. Both processes occurred in the mind. However, one happens from obtaining information into your subconscious and the other occurs from an innate ability to believe in yourself, no matter what is going on.

Every human is heading towards a goal. For many people, these goals were induced by someone or something. What you feed into your mind is exactly what your mind is going to process. This culminates into how we interact with our environment. For example, a brilliant child who was brought up in an environment where he had no time to study and thus hardly had passing grades may be told over and over that he's stupid. As a result, his mind would have been programmed to believing this— even though it is a lie.

Without a conscious effort to understanding the source of the negative belief and reprogramming his mind with a more positive one —he might never be able to maximize his true potential. If you can relate to this, maybe even about your height or appearance, then you must reprogram your mind.

Your mind may have been subconsciously programmed for you, but it's time you take up the challenge and do something about it. Do you want to go through life living out someone else's ignorant statements about you? You might be subconsciously striving to attain goals that some persons unconsciously set for you. Sometimes it can be intentional and cruel, but most times, it's usually done ignorantly as the society does not understand the intricacies of the subconscious. To reprogram your mind, you have to consciously decide your aspiration and prepare your mind to gun for that goal. This will create the new image and representation of yourself in your memory, which is the privy of the subconscious. When the subconscious accesses your memory, it now sees you as the new image and then begins to transform you into that image almost effortlessly. If you chase goals that are not really yours, you might struggle and may end up exasperated at your lack of success and satisfaction. It's time to act and time to speak to yourself! You need to reprogram your mind to get things done. Just like the saying, *"you get back what you give to life"*

YOU ARE A CREATOR

God created man in his own image therefore we are God-like and possesses his awesome qualities. One major and distinct quality of God is creativity. The idea you have to create an object, business or become an artist (singer, actor, dancer, etc.) is not a coincidence. God placed it in your mind and consequently, he will equip you with all you need to get it done. Have you noticed that special quality and ability which he has placed in your heart never leaves? It's always there waiting for you to act on it. (God is waiting for you to act. He cannot move until you move)

Have you noticed how beautifully and fearlessly children learn to do things. Innocent and naïve as they are, they never give up in their pursuits, regardless of the number of times they fall and hurt themselves —they always get right up. There is no fear of failure in their hearts— this is the fundamental difference between the approach of kids and that of adults to achieving their goals. God still speaks to you as he did when you were a kid, however you are now fearful of the world, and your mind is clouded by your many negative experiences. Remember, your experiences are not you —they are just things you did or passed through. You don't have to let all these negative experiences weigh you down. If you do not act, no one will do it for you. A lot of people have taken charge of their lives and are now doing well and achieving their dreams. How does it feel imagining yourself in that same position you've always dreamt of? How do you think it will feel fulfilling your long term dreams and seeing everything work out perfectly for you?

If you don't like your current situation, then create the one you want. You have the power to do it. Many times you hear people complain about their present life situation but do nothing about it. The situation will not change if something is not done to change it. The first step to changing any state is by embracing it. Instead of wallowing in self-denial, you have to be truthful to yourself and face the reality of where you are and say, *"Maybe I can learn something from this situation."* You will gain strength and patience once you accept it. This will then propel you to creating a path way to changing your state. This is the most strategic point in any change process. You are right where you are supposed to be. It is time! Do not wait any longer! Begin to create! Explore all your senses and create an actionable and pragmatic plan. Miles Munroe said *"a gift is the inherent capacity to fulfill a function that meets a need in creation."*

BE STILL AND KNOW THAT I AM GOD

I plead with you to take part in this very short exercise. It will only take less than five minutes of your time. Go to a quiet place, standstill, and shut your mind off your environment. What do you hear? The answer is nothing. Absolute tranquility fills the room.

This goes to show that you can be a blank canvas just so you can create a work of art — whatever life you want. But this cannot happen unless you are still. Your mind cannot operate in maximum capacity with so much chaos going on around it. Being still translates to the mind, body, and everything around you being in harmony. Shutting your mind off might be difficult but prayers or meditation can assist you. When you successfully achieve it, you will be able to hear the instructions. Listen closely, and you will eventually hear. Stop thinking and doing so much.

We tend to think that the more we move, the more we accomplish. This is not true. Sometimes we do not accomplishing anything at all with all the motion. Toiling is not the answer — it is exhausting, unpleasant and uninspiring. To be uninspired means to have no intellectual, emotional, or spiritual excitement; lacking spirit or creativity. I'm sure most of us can relate. The quickest way to the grave is to work this way. Even if you are earning a lot of money, you won't enjoy it. What you should be focused on is acting on what God placed in your heart. So, why continue on with life in this state of being? Of course, you have to pay bills, take care of loved ones, but you do not have to live your entire life that way. When you have time off from work, spend time alone —even if it is for a couple of hours. Also, spend time marveling at nature's awesome creation such as the ocean, the forest, the sky, and this will serve as an awesome routine for inspiration.

WORK WITH A PURPOSE

Irrespective of your background, faith or belief, there is always an inner spiritual strength that gives your work a purpose. Working with purpose fulfills deep human desire to create in accordance with a belief system and long term goal. When you get to understand what your purpose is and break out of the mold — you enjoy the freedom and joy of inner satisfaction that comes with working on things that resonates with yourself.

Don't get me wrong, there is nothing wrong with hard work. In fact, it is a necessity. It teaches us discipline, structure and endurance. But, there is a cogent need to focus your hard work on your purpose. When the time comes, you will be prepared because you endured those rough days and long hours.

There are days when you want to throw in the towel and give up. "*What is it all for?*" you ask. It is preparing you for your destiny. This very moment, you are walking in, GO! In the book 'The Alchemist' it says, *"There is only one way to learn. It's through action. Everything you need to know, you have learned through your journey."* Once you discover your passion, don't wait any longer, or life will pass you by. There are several people out there working to make ends meet, and before you know it, they are gone. Honestly, do you think they are working because they like it? This is very sad because some of these people are our parents or grandparents. If you are like me, I am sure you want to help take care of them. And it feels almost paralyzing to know you cannot help your loved ones because you too are struggling to take of yourself and your family. This is the story of many people across the world who have entrusted the system with their time and commitment — and not receiving a return on their investment.

They have given most of their lives to a company and have little to nothing to show for it but resentment, health problems, and stress. I am sure they would have preferred to do something fulfilling and purposeful.

HAVE FAITH

Faith is a strong or unshakable belief in something —especially without proof or evidence. In this sense, it means believing that, one day, you will actually be doing that very thing you envision. Of course, it's in your mind because that is where everything starts. You have to envisage it until you can actually see it! Faith makes up for your expectations with hope. And what does hope mean? Hope is the feeling that we can get what we wish or that events or circumstances will turn out for the best. Therefore, faith is the matter, the consistency; what gives weight to what we desire or wish we could have. It is the proof of things we cannot see physically. It is our assurance that even though our eyes do not behold it, it is reality.

Faith involves doing something every day that moves you closer in the direction of your vision. This is called actionable faith. The bible says that faith without works is dead. Without investing efforts in your vision, even when it seems unclear, you cannot be said to have faith. Faith is action based. It has to be proven. When you possess it, you will see the physical manifestation of what you have been wanting for in no time.

According to Dr. Alan Watts, a popular British writer and philosopher of the 20th century, irrevocable (unalterable) commitment to any religion is not only intellectual suicide; it is positive unfaith as it closes the mind to any new vision of the world. Faith is above all, openness, an act of trust in the unknown. Faith also entails being obedient and acting on the gift or gifts that were placed inside of you. Do you think that people like Oprah Winfrey, Bill Gates, and Warren Buffet worry about missing church or paying tithes? No! I'm sure you hear about these people helping people who are in need, giving to charities, etc. Your passion or dreams are not restricted or limited to education, religious beliefs, or a particular job.

WHAT DO YOU REALLY WANT TO BE?

Be honest with yourself as to what you wanted to be when you were a kid. Most of the time, we don't even realize how we end up at the job we're at or our current situations. Many of us are probably in places where we never imagined for ourselves. You probably have an amazing gift, and you are wasting time in someone's office pushing paper several hours a week. You could be at home putting those hours into your own project that could really change the world.

When you were a child, God spoke to you in the form of friends or family and told you exactly what you were supposed to be. My granddad always used to tell me I would be some kind of businessman because my parents dressed me in suits all the time. Friends told me I had a knack for writing. I took their observations with a pinch of salt, because as a child following in my older brother's footsteps, I was trying to play sports.

Somewhere along the line we get side tracked. Many times, it is because of some very nonfactual comments said to us by some people. They tell us about our limitations and how it would hinder us from accomplishing our dreams. Then we agree and settle for an easier route. Or we settle for something we merely like instead of something we are passionate about. That which we are passionate about doing, even without pay, is most times our destiny. Even if we decide to follow other paths, what we fail to realize is that, what's in our hearts are from God — they will never go away. This is why we find ourselves still doing these things on the side but not maximizing it. Passions never die; you either maximize it or waste it. Either way, it remains with you.

Stop listening to those negative voices in your mind or those of people in your life saying you can't do it. They have been indoctrinated into the worldly system of thinking.

God is capable of much more, however it is you who holds the key. Don't limit God. Don't limit yourself.

THE POWER IN YOU

Each and every person walking this earth is capable of greatness. Inherent in us is a magnificent power that gives us the ability to do all we can imagine and even more. What are you afraid of? Success? When you refuse to try, that is failure guaranteed.

A mistake is another opportunity to succeed. The more you try, the more you learn something different about yourself that will prepare you for your destiny. No matter how bleak your situation is, remember there is always a way out. Remember the story of Joseph, who was sold into slavery by his own brothers, then thrown into prison. As if things could not get any worse, he was close to being killed after being accused of sleeping with Potiphar's wife. He focused his attention on the good instead of how terrible it seemed on the surface. He created a way out of no way. He used his vision to speak life into the prisoners, pharaoh's men, and pharaoh himself. He ultimately became the King of Egypt.

I have seen a lot of situations similar to Joseph's. There have been cases where the victim started out in the system from childhood to adulthood. Even if you find yourself in such unfortunate circumstances, the power to change is still in you. Many times, we feel that we would arrive at our destination through a direct route. Life is not a linear equation. The power in you means that there is something you possess that can take you a step further to where you aim to be. Keep taking baby steps. Keep moving forward. The power in you will ensure that you never get stranded.

YOU CAN BE WHATEVER YOU WANT

You can be whatever it is you desire; a director, CEO, singer, actor, dancer, astronaut, doctor, lawyer, etc. Whatever it is you want, you can do it. It's going to take a vision, creativity, effort, hard work, and belief. Anything worth something is going to take work and discipline. Nothing is going to fall out of the sky. It has to start within you. You have to see it, believe it, and then achieve it as Napoleon Hill said *"your dreams are worth everything"*. Even worth more than that large lump sum of money you have. That is only temporary. Your dreams are forever.

A big issue militating against dreaming big is the lack of vision. This is because we only see as far as our eyes allow us. That is when our minds have to take over. The late founder and CEO of Apple Steve Jobs encouraged us to DREAM BIG, not see big. However, they go hand in hand because you have to train your mind to focus on those things you desire.

Seeing starts with the eyes but vision starts with the imagination. Both take place in the mind —the most powerful tool ever created. According to Albert Einstein, *"Imagination is more important than knowledge. Imagination is the language of the soul. Pay attention to your imagination and you will discover all you need to be fulfilled."* Search for what you want without having someone else directing you. Don't wait for something drastic to happen. I am positive someone you know has what you are searching for, or they know someone that can help you get it.

CONFIRMATION

Confirmation is a corroborative statement or piece of evidence. It is the validation or confirmation of the potency of a dream or passion by an external body. This could be a song, a happening or a person who has no worldly idea of what your dreams are. Everything in the universe has already conspired with your spirit to make it happen once you make up your mind about what you want to do. The universe is working on your behalf. There are no coincidences. You have to listen and pay close attention to everything. I mean everything and everywhere.

A good friend of mine was searching for a career in talk show hosting. She was told that she could not find what she was searching for at a sports bar or club because those are not good or 'Godly' places. Thankfully, she did not listen to those close-minded people. She ended up signing with a well-known label at a club and is now hosting her own internet talk show. If you think that you missed out on your dream or someone else took your dream — you are mistaken. You have been specifically crafted for your dream, and it has been specifically crafted for you. It has always been there waiting for you since you were born. There are no deadlines or punishments if you don't see it right away. Dr. Watts states that genuine love comes from knowledge — not duty or guilt. It will always reappear again. When it does, I hope you live the life of your dreams this time.

When confirmation comes, you will know. God send confirmations to you to assure you that he's got your back. Like I said in the beginning of the book, I got a confirmation to write this book via a YouTube video.

WHAT IF IT DOESN'T WORK?

Oh my God, it did not work! I am a failure! Most times, when we finally build up the courage to pursue our dreams, it does not work out exactly as we planned it. When this happens, we start to doubt ourselves again. We ask ourselves if it is really what we're supposed to do. The reason it did not work out is probably because of poor planning. This is not the time to give up or wallow in self-pity. Instead, pick up the pieces and correct your wrongs. We should try falling forward without fear. But, it all starts with a vision and a plan.

Sometimes, things are going to happen that are out of our control, but we have to respond accordingly and take control of our lives. Do not allow the situation to take control of you. Always look for the good in it. There is always a good, even in the worst situations. An opportunity of a lifetime is waiting for you. Change your attitude!

There are cases where people burnt all bridges in pursuit of their dreams and came out victorious. Pay attention to some poor people who come from nothing and don't have anything. They are hungry. They work harder. I'm sure you've heard of putting all your marbles in a basket. While I was preparing for an NFL combine at a facility in Atlanta, GA., there were several guys there who had been out of the game for a while and some who did not have a college education. Some of the trainers would laugh at them because they had a minute chance of being selected by an NFL team. Even with the half chance, they were still 'putting all their marbles in a basket'. They were the guys who worked the hardest not caring about the results as long as they put their all into it. There was one guy in particular who received attention from NFL Scouts. He was one of the guys the trainers laughed at. He was ex-military and was one of the strongest and fastest guys there. When he walked through the door, you saw the focus on his face. He was there for one thing —only to make it. On the other hand, I wanted it the same as he did but in the back of my mind, I was thinking, "I want this really bad but if I don't make it, I have a college degree, and I will find a good job one day." Somehow I thought I was better than those guys because they did not have a degree. Instead of living in the moment and taking advantage of an opportunity of a lifetime, I was thinking of the possibility of failure and my chance at a back-up plan. And it turned out exactly the way I was thinking. I was eventually discovered by an Arena II team but not an NFL team. Instead of focusing all my attention on being discovered by an NFL Team, I was still searching for jobs, and I limited my vision to the gym.

The most important point from this story is the idea of limiting our vision to a particular place. In that situation, I was limiting my vision to the time spent in the gym instead of carrying it around all the time. Most great athletes leave the gym, and they are still reading the play book, working out after practice. We limit our visions to the system mindset or a place most of the time.

If it doesn't work, keep trying. When we actually do step out of our comfort zone, it's not always going to work for whatever reason. If it does not fall through, that doesn't mean it's not going to work. Go back to the drawing board. You are destined to do this! This is who you are! It's waiting for you! Remember, you are not waiting for anyone or anything (because we were always told to wait on the Lord). It already exists, and it's waiting for you to realize it. Once you realize that, your life will become more meaningful.

FINAL THOUGHTS

There is more to life than the little luxury enjoyable from paid jobs. There is a lot more in store for you only if you are bold enough to defy the system man created. If you still put all your trust in this confining system, you are sadly mistaken and limiting yourself. Better yet, you are limiting GOD. There is so much more to life than just surviving so that you can one day go to heaven. Life is not all about money; however, money creates opportunity for you to create opportunities for yourself and others. This is how the process should go. One of my favorite bible scriptures, Genesis 12:2, states, "I will make you into a great nation and I will bless you; I will make your name great, and you will be a blessing". At first I took this scripture at face value but when I began to meditate on it, I saw the true meaning. Nation means your family or legacy.

The Hilton Family created a foundation for generations to come so that their family will never have to work a day in their lives. When you think of Hilton, you think of a great service for people across the world. The Hilton brand also creates employment opportunities for thousands across the world. He had a vision and he manifested it. He used his God complex and created a legacy so that his name could live on forever. We all have that same complex. We just have to use it.

Take a chance, it won't hurt. The worse thing that could happen is you! What I mean is that you are the only thing standing in your way. When you allow people or circumstances to get in your way, you are giving them more power than the God within you. The bible talks about power to trample over serpents. What the writers of the bible actually meant was power over doubt, fear, worry, stress, anxiety, death, negative people, etc. The scripture finishes with the statement with: "absolutely nothing will harm you".

The most wonderful thing about this life is that it's an UNKNOWN journey. And somehow we feel like we need to be SAVED from it. If we are living our lives in fear, there is no way love can be involved. There is nothing that can SAVE you from the life God has given you. You can make good decisions or bad decisions, but things are still going to happen. Also, you can't escape death because it's a part of life. Life and death coexist and death is inevitable. When we stop fearing death and the unknown, we will be able to truly live.

Most of the distractions in our lives are temporary gratification or nostalgia to make you feel good in hopes of delaying the inevitable (which is dealing with your true self). Focus less on searching for temporary fixes in relationships, church, medicine, drugs, and other institutions. Instead, focus your attention more on your true, powerful, already great self. Therein lies all the answers you are searching for! BELIEVE IN YOU!

Most people wait until they reach a low point in life before they search for or rediscover their greatness. I believe it's never too late, but why the wait? I used the term rediscover intentionally because the greatness has always been there. As a child, we realized our greatness but along the way, fear crept in causing us to doubt who we really are. Instead, we began a lifelong search for something other than who we are. Not knowing that greatness already dwells in us.

What I have realized is that we are actually in conflict with ourselves —trying to get back to our true self without letting go of the new self. Throughout our lives, we have been taught that we were born sinners and that we need to be saved. The blatant truth is that, we were born great and have been deceived into believing the opposite. That is why we yearn for a certain status in positions at jobs or certain feelings in drugs, religion, and other things. We constantly try to get back to somewhere, but we don't quite know who or what we are trying to get back to.

Some even equate this with the journey to heaven. All our lives, we have been manipulated and confused into thinking we are inferior. This has made us lose every ounce of hope in US and put all of it in someone else or some other place —in a paradise far off that's full of the beauty and greatness we desire. What we forget is just like we imagine heaven to be this amazing, extraordinary place; we have the power to transcend into this paradise while on earth. Better still, we have the power to create a heaven for ourselves on earth. Why do we have to spend our lives waiting to die before we experience paradise? This mindset has led us to a state of disbelief in ourselves to the point where we give up very easily. Please take a look in the mirror right now and search no more. You have found that the greatness you are searching for and it is you. You are God personified!

The system is failing right before our eyes. The relationship that exists between God and us is symbiotic. Therefore, he needs us and we need him also. We can never be separated. Don't allow anyone or anything to stop you from going after your dreams. You can do it! Keep trusting, keep moving, you are almost there.

CPSIA information can be obtained
at www.ICGtesting.com
Printed in the USA
LVHW020548160421
684696LV00019B/1235